Frances Folsom Cleveland

Frances Folsom Cleveland

✦★✦★✦★✦★✦★✦★✦★✦★✦★✦✦

1864–1947

BY SUSAN SINNOTT

CHILDREN'S PRESS®
A Division of Grolier Publishing
New York London Hong Kong Sydney
Danbury, Connecticut

Consultants: CARL SFERRAZZA ANTHONY
Historical researcher and author of First Ladies: The Saga of the
Presidents' Wives and Their Power; *historical consultant to the
Smithsonian Institution's First Ladies exhibit*
LINDA CORNWELL
Learning Resource Consultant
Indiana Department of Education

Project Editor: DOWNING PUBLISHING SERVICES
Page Layout: CAROLE DESNOES
Photo Researcher: JAN IZZO

Visit Children's Press on the Internet at:
http://publishing.grolier.com

Library of Congress Cataloging-in-Publication Data
Sinnott, Susan
     Frances Folsom Cleveland 1864–1947 / by Susan Sinnott
       p. cm. — (Encyclopedia of first ladies)
     Includes bibliographical references and index.
     Summary: Presents a biography of the wife of the man who was both the twenty-second
and twenty-fourth president of the United States, the first bride of a president to be married
in the White House.
     ISBN 0-516-20476-9
     1. Cleveland, Frances Folsom. 1864–1947—Juvenile literature. 2. Presidents' spouses—
United States—Biography—Juvenile literature. [1. Cleveland, Frances Folsom 1864–1947.
2. First ladies. 3. Women—Biography.] I. Title II. Series.
E697.5. S56   1998
973.8'5'092—dc21   98–7895
[B]   CIP
                                                                   AC

Table of Contents

Frances Folsom Cleveland

CHAPTER ONE

A White House Wedding

★ ★ ★ ★ ★ ★ ★ ★ ★ ★ ★ ★ ★ ★ ★ ★

Once President Grover Cleveland made the official announcement of his engagement to Miss Frances Folsom, everyone in the country began to behave like anxious wedding guests. The ceremony was to take place on June 2, 1886—only a week away —and the public craved news of every wedding detail: Was it true that a whole army of florists had been engaged to hang bowers of roses and pansies throughout the White House's Blue Room? And what about orchids—were they really to be brought in by the cartful? Was the bridal gown to be trimmed in orange blossoms? And, at only twenty-one, is "Frankie," as every-

★ ★ ★ ★ ★ ★ ★ ★ ★ ★ ★ ★ ★ ★ ★ ★

one called her, really up to the demands of being a First Lady? Can she truly be in love with Grover Cleveland, who's not at all handsome and nearly twenty-eight years older than she? What *does* she see in him?

Americans felt justified in their desperate search for information. After all, it was their wedding, too wasn't it? It would be the first to take place in *their* house, the White House. And, if Grover Cleveland wasn't

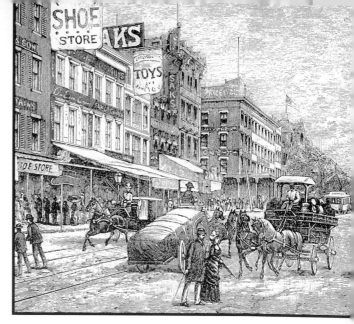

Seventh Street NW, Washington, D.C., as it looked in the late 1800s

A view of Pennsylvania Avenue at Vernon Row, Washington, D.C., at about the time Frances Folsom married President Grover Cleveland

Most visitors to the White House in the 1880s and 1890s arrived on foot, on horseback, or in horse-drawn carriages.

exactly everyone's idea of an affable family member, sweet Frances Folsom would make any parent proud.

No one, it seemed, could resist her warmth and charm. A White House staff member remembered her arrival at the mansion early on the morning of her wedding, emerging from her carriage excitedly and greeting everyone with a huge smile. Then, he recalled, Frankie ". . . tripped up the steps and swept through the great entrance like a radiant vision of young springtime."

All this press attention irritated President Cleveland tremendously. He

Nothing New: The Power of the Press

✫ ✫

Grover Cleveland's frustration with reporters sounds familiar to modern ears. However, in his day, the power of the American press was just gathering steam. In 1865, about 500 daily newspapers circulated to 2 million readers around the country. Their front pages—called tombstones—carried dense columns of small type, unbroken by pictures or headlines. They lost money. Over the next thirty years, new printing and illustrating technologies, a growing population of readers, and advertisers with money to spend contributed to a new type of journalism. By 1900, 2,000 daily newspapers gave 15 million eager Americans the news. Leading the charge was Joseph Pulitzer, a Hungarian immigrant who had purchased the failing *New York World* in 1883. While Pulitzer demanded exacting accuracy from his reporters, he used his paper to expose the evils of the day: political corruption, ill-gotten wealth, and poverty. Using banner headlines, Sunday supplements, promotions, and even the first comics, he attracted both readers and advertisers. Ironically, by running a scathing story about Cleveland's 1884 presidential opponent James Blaine, Pulitzer and the *World* helped to catapult Cleveland into office. The power of the press, for better or worse, had been firmly established.

begrudged reporters—those "ghouls," as he called them—any look at his private life. When presented with evidence of leaks about the wedding or honeymoon, the president's eyes would bulge and his face would become very red. He didn't want his wife to be a symbol of *anything*—not youth, beauty, or romance. Grover just wanted an ordinary American housewife—even if the "house" was the White House!

While Grover Cleveland fretted about his "poor girl," Frankie seemed almost amused by the attention. Why less than a year earlier, she'd been a

Former First Lady Lucretia Garfield (above) left a small embroidered pillow in an upstairs bedroom of the White House.

being copied: her hairstyle, the way she tilted her head in photographs, even her habit of tucking a few flowers into the waistband of her dress. Who could have imagined it?

Just after Frank, as her family referred to her, arrived at the White House on the morning of June 2, she was escorted by one of Grover's sisters to a second-floor bedroom. There, amidst vases of fresh-cut roses, she spent the rest of the day preparing for the seven o'clock ceremony. As she stood before Dolley Madison's own mirror and straightened her white bridal gown and fifteen-foot train, she must have felt the presence of the other First Ladies. The room was said to have been a particular favorite of Julia Grant's. And didn't that small embroidered pillow have the initials "L.G." for Lucretia Garfield? Did their stomachs flutter, too, she wondered, as they waited to make their entrances?

At exactly seven, John Philip Sousa lifted his baton and the scarlet-uniformed Marine Band began Mendelssohn's "Wedding March." Frankie took the president's arm and together they descended the grand

normal college student from Buffalo, New York! Now her pretty face and wavy chestnut hair were seen in pictures and drawings in many national newspapers. Everything about her was

13

John Philip Sousa (1854–1932)

✫ ✫

Known as the March King, musician and bandleader John Philip Sousa composed some of America's most beloved—and hummable—music. Guided by the belief that "a march should make a man with a wooden leg step out," Sousa composed about 140 lively marches during his career. His most famous is perhaps "The Stars and Stripes Forever," that toe-tapping tune we know from so many Fourth of July fireworks displays. As a child, Sousa played both trombone and violin. In 1880, after several years as a performer, he became director of the Marine Band that played at the Cleveland-Folsom wedding. He soon began composing. Then, in 1892, in an era when band concerts were America's favorite entertainment, he formed his own band and toured the country. His patriotic style reflected the nation's self-confident mood at the turn of the century and earned him wealth and success. He went on to take over the navy bands during World War I and wrote ten comic operas, three novels, and an autobiography entitled *Marching Along*.

John Philip Sousa   *Sousa and the Marine Band*

Here Comes the Bride

✶ ✶

For Americans, the wedding of Grover Cleveland and Frances Folsom came as close to a royal wedding as anything. It represented the height of fashion, glittering with elegance and excess. During this period—called Victorian after powerful Queen Victoria of Great Britain—many modern bridal traditions began. Although some Victorian brides still decked themselves in gowns of richly colored fabric, the frothy white wedding gown had gained popularity since Queen Victoria wore one in 1840. Frances's dress was no exception. Its full bustle (a pad or framework to support yards of material draped at the back of the skirt), flowing train, and long, lacy veil enveloped her elegantly. Queen Victoria also made orange blossoms a must for bridal bouquets and other adornment; indeed, Frances trimmed her gown with the fragrant blooms. For decorations, Victorians loved flow-

The Cleveland-Folsom wedding

ers of all varieties. They even developed an elaborate "language of flowers," assigning a specific meaning to each. A gentleman said "I love you" to a lady with a red rose and hoped she would respond with purple pansies, which meant "You occupy my thoughts." Masses of roses and pansies decorated the Blue Room for the Cleveland-Folsom nuptials.

On the evening of Frances Folsom's marriage to President Grover Cleveland, a crowd of people waited outside the White House hoping to get a glimpse of the bride.

staircase, unattended. They stood in the shimmering Blue Room with their twenty-eight guests just long enough to exchange wedding vows. As they headed into the State Dining Room, a twenty-one-gun salute boomed from the Navy Yard and church bells rang throughout the city.

For one night, anyway, the White House was a fairy-tale castle. A beautiful princess, dressed in yards and yards of creamy white satin, took the arm of the king and became a glowing queen. The magic would disappear soon enough—everyone knew it—but for this one moment, the world was a very special place. And Frances Folsom Cleveland had captured its heart.

Portrait of America, 1864: A Troubled Year

✶ ✶

As Frank Clara Folsom was born in 1864, the Civil War ground into its last year. By then, the United States included thirty-six war-weary states and nearly 35 million people (including the eleven states of the seceded South). Nevada joined the Union as a free state in October.

In the spring of 1864, the North put its hopes of winning in the hands of General Ulysses S. Grant. As the new commander of all Union troops, he hoped to make short work of the failing Confederacy. But 1864 proved a difficult year for Grant. In his push to capture Richmond, Virginia, he lost 60,000 men (including 12,000 in one day at the battle of Cold Harbor) and gained little. Grant finally outwaited the enemy in a siege at Petersburg that lasted into 1865.

In the Deep South, however, General William Tecumseh Sherman marched triumphantly into Atlanta and then on to the sea at Savannah, Georgia. President Abraham Lincoln, running for a second term that year, got the boost he needed. Union morale rose as Atlanta fell, and Lincoln won easily. Union victory would not be far behind, coming finally in April 1865.

American bloodshed that year was not limited to the Civil War. Conflict of another kind was brewing out West. To make way for pioneers, the government herded Native Americans onto smaller and smaller reservations. But the Indians were hunters and needed to follow the buffalo and game to live. Tension and disorder on the Great Plains increased, punctuated by uneasy peace and broken treaties. Then, in 1864, American soldiers slaughtered more than three hundred Cheyenne and Arapaho; most of them women and children. They were encamped on the banks of Sand Creek outside Denver, Colorado, where their leader, Black Kettle, had just attended a peace conference. In the coming years, more violence would end native lifeways forever.

CHAPTER TWO

Buffalo Beginnings

✶ ✶ ✶ ✶ ✶ ✶ ✶ ✶ ✶ ✶ ✶ ✶ ✶ ✶ ✶

Grover Cleveland and Oscar Folsom were old Buffalo friends and, eventually, law partners. They worked hard and played hard, spending days in their busy law offices and nights in Buffalo's lively saloons. Grover could remember when, still in his twenties, he would stay up all night drinking beer and dancing in one of his favorite "halls," usually in Buffalo's rougher neighborhoods. Then at dawn, he'd head for his office, where he'd splash water on his face, drink several cups of coffee, and prepare for the day's work. His tirelessness was truly legendary.

Even after Oscar Folsom married Emma Harmon,

✶ ✶ ✶ ✶ ✶ ✶ ✶ ✶ ✶ ✶ ✶ ✶ ✶ ✶ ✶

Grover Cleveland's law office in Buffalo, New York

the two men continued their lively socializing. Grover liked late nights around a saloon table. Oscar, on the other hand, loved fast carriage rides and wild adventures. It was only on July 21, 1864, when Emma Folsom gave birth to the couple's first child, Frank Clara, that Oscar settled down—at least a little. ("Frank" was indeed the baby girl's given name; it was legally changed to the more feminine "Frances" many years later.)

Grover Cleveland, too, was moved by the birth of his friend's child. "Uncle Cleve" was one of the tiny girl's first visitors, and he gave her a

A view of Buffalo as it looked in the mid-nineteenth century, when Grover Cleveland and Oscar Folsom were law partners there

New York, U.S.A.

✶ ✶

New York stretches from the Atlantic Ocean west to the Great Lakes and north to Canada. The great metropolis of New York City, the state's front door, occupies its southernmost corner, while lovely farmlands and forests cover most of its 47,000 square miles (121,730 square kilometers). Between 1825 and the 1850s, New Yorkers built the Erie Canal and the railroad to connect New York City with Buffalo, 400 miles (644 km) away on the other side of the state. On the shores of Lake Erie and at the edge of the western frontier, Buffalo became the state's back door. When Frank Folsom was born there in 1864, the city bustled with commerce and industry as goods and people came and went between the East Coast and points west. Tourists thronged to Niagara Falls, some 20 miles (32 km) away, to see daredevils dance across

Niagara Falls

them on high-tension wires. In the 1860s, honeymooners, too, were just beginning to discover the romance of those thundering waters. Mid-nineteenth-century New York bristled with more-serious activities as well. A strong antislavery state, New York sent more soldiers—nearly 450,000—to Civil War battlefields than any other state and was an important stopping point on the Underground Railroad. Indeed, former slaves Sojourner Truth, an activist for abolition, and Harriet Tubman, who helped hundreds of slaves to freedom, both lived in New York State.

Frank Folsom spent her childhood summers at Folsomdale, the home of her grand-parents.

handsome baby carriage. Only twenty-seven and very ambitious, Grover was content to put off marriage and father-hood, at least for the time being. By 1870, Cleveland was active in the Democratic Party, served as sheriff of Erie Country, and was already talked about for higher office—perhaps even the governorship of New York State!

Frank enjoyed a happy, pampered childhood, far away from the rough-and-tumble world of politics. She was very close to her gentle mother and adored by her fun-loving father. Frank particularly loved the long summers spent at Folsomdale, the nearby coun-try home of her grandparents. There, she and Oscar—whose passion for wild games and fast races she shared—liked to ride in a carriage behind a par-ticularly fast-trotting horse. Their laughs and shrieks could be heard across the countryside.

Frank and Emma would often spend the entire summer at Folsom-dale, while Oscar attended to business back in Buffalo. At Folsomdale, packs of cousins roamed the fields and orchards. For Frank, this was a won-derful relief from being an only child. (A younger sister, Nellie, died in infancy.)

All the children especially enjoyed the visits of Frank's friend, Uncle Cleve. Mr. Cleveland, they could tell, really liked children. The cousins par-ticularly enjoyed the times he joined them in the apple orchards, where they all played a rollicking game of pitch the apple.

John Folsom, Frank's grandfather

Clara Hernden Folsom, Frank's grandmother

Back in Buffalo in the fall, Frank attended first Madame Breckner's French Kindergarten, then Miss Bissel's School for Young Ladies. She loved school, as much for the company of friends as for the academics. She was liked everywhere she went. When, in July of 1875, she celebrated her eleventh birthday with her beloved parents, it seemed the path to future happiness was brightly lit.

The day after her birthday, she and her mother traveled to Medina, New York, about 40 miles (64 km) east of Buffalo, to spend a few weeks with Emma's mother, Ruth Harmon. As usual, Oscar stayed behind in Buffalo. Frank loved her kindhearted Grandmother Ruth and looked forward to visiting her cheerful home. It was probably for the best that she and her mother were there when they received the terrible news.

On Friday evening, July 23, Oscar Folsom was riding in a buggy, fast—too fast—as he so often did. The

23

Where Children Could Grow

★ ★

The concept of the "kindergarten," or children's garden, was born in Germany in the 1830s. This new approach to education was based on the revolutionary idea that children learned by playing rather than by memorizing and reciting. For a long time, children had been viewed and treated as little adults without special needs of their own. Now, kindergartens gave four- to six-year-olds a place where they could "unfold naturally, like flowers." Individual kindergartens (like Madame Breckner's French Kindergarten) began to appear in the United States in the 1850s. In 1873, St. Louis was the first to incorporate them into the school system. Today, nearly 4 million children attend kindergarten in the United States.

wheels of the buggy skidded, and he was thrown into the street. He died instantly of massive head injuries. Frank would never forget the terrible night when she sat at the top of her grandmother's staircase and watched as an uncle tried to hold the lantern so her mother could read the telegram from Buffalo. Her mother's desperate sobs lasted through the night.

The next few days were a blur. Emma and Frank returned quickly to Buffalo, where the funeral was held. Then Frank returned to Medina to stay with Grandmother Ruth, while Emma Folsom went to Folsomdale to console

Oscar's father. A little later, Oscar's will was read. He'd left Emma a $5,000 insurance policy and a tangled mess of financial dealings. Fortunately, the court appointed Grover Cleveland to administer his friend's estate. Grover knew that Emma and Frank's futures depended on his responsible management of their finances. He became Emma's trusted adviser and Frank's unofficial guardian.

Grover felt his first duty was to try to help Emma build a stable life in Buffalo. Frank was enrolled again at Miss Bissel's and was just about to resume her studies when Emma received an invitation she couldn't refuse. Emma's sister Nellie had married former British captain T. R. Huddleston, and he was now practicing law in St. Paul, Minnesota. They lived in a very large house, and Nellie was anxious for Emma and Frank to come live with them. Emma, whose terrible loneliness may have clouded her judgment, accepted the invitation.

In the late summer of 1876, Emma and Frank boarded the train for the long ride to St. Paul. Frank began attending the Wheaton School, a fine all-girls' academy. She quickly made friends and was happier there than she'd ever expected to be in a strange new city. The happiness in the Huddleston family, however, did not last long. Nellie and T. R. fought constantly, and the captain's terrible rages made everyone's home life a nightmare. Within six months, Emma decided she could no longer live in the midst of her sister's stormy marriage. She pulled Frank out of Wheaton and returned to Grandmother Ruth's home in Medina.

A view of St. Paul, Minnesota, as it looked when Emma and Frank Folsom lived there with Emma's sister Nellie and Nellie's husband, T. R. Huddleston

Grover Cleveland

Frank Folsom began attending Wells College in February 1882.

Nellie divorced Captain Huddleston and returned to Medina as well. Emma Folsom needed to face rebuilding her life once again and so she sought the advice of Grover Cleveland. She was pleased to learn that he had been watching Oscar's estate closely and had made several wise and profitable investments. Emma was soon able to buy a home in Buffalo and enroll Frank at one of the city's finest schools.

By the time Frank was sixteen, her social life had become so lively that her grades began to fall. Emma worried about her daughter's distracted state of mind. She was somewhat relieved when Frank's Latin teacher noted that the girl is "a great favorite with her classmates . . . at recess or between study hours the boys always surrounded her and she seemed to enjoy their society. She was not a flirt by any means and had a great deal of dignity about her."

At seventeen, pretty Frank Folsom was engaged to one of Buffalo's most handsome bachelors, Charles Townsend. The news was not altogether welcome: Emma wanted her daughter to finish high school, at least, and Grover Cleveland insisted the funds were available for college after that. Frank and Charles were engaged for less than a year when Frank herself began to have doubts. She finally wrote to Charles that she didn't believe in her heart he was the right man for her. She knew she wasn't yet mature enough to make such an important decision.

Frank never returned to her high school after breaking her engagement to Charles Townsend. Instead, she received a certificate of completion, which allowed her to apply for college admission. In February 1882, she was admitted to Wells College in Aurora, New York, and began attending classes almost immediately.

A Proper Lady

✫ ✫

The road to educational equality for women has been a long one. In the nineteenth century, while more and more girls attended college, it was still largely felt that education should prepare them for marriage, not a career. For years, men suspected that the study of academics might render women unsuitable for marriage and make them abandon their proper roles as wives and mothers. Therefore, etiquette, home economics, and the arts were popular subjects for women to study. Didn't a young woman of refinement who displayed the correct manners have a much better chance of attracting an acceptable husband? Outside the classroom, much of America, too, was obsessed by proper behavior, believing that it set the higher classes apart from the lower. Hundreds of books advised readers about "agreeable" manners, etiquette at the table, polite conversation, acceptable conduct in public, and attractive personal appearance. Sample these "laws" from an 1879 etiquette book: "Never exaggerate. Never laugh at the misfortunes of others. Upon rising, take a complete bath. Avoid undue haste and excitement while traveling. Never leave the table with food in the mouth." And, for husbands and wives, "Always use the most gentle and loving words when addressing each other." Good advice, all.

CHAPTER THREE

Cause Célèbre

* * * * * * * * * * * * * * * *

Frank, now often called Frances, had worried a bit that the other students at Wells College would be too worldly, even snobbish. Her fears, however, were put to rest as soon as she moved into the large, comfortable house that she would share with the twenty-one other members of the freshman class. She wrote to her mother that even though the atmosphere was a bit "refined," she truly loved college life.

At Wells, Frances quickly learned, rules of decorum were strictly observed. The training of a proper lady, according to Dean Helen Fairchild Smith, was one of the hallmarks of a Wells education. A nod or a glare

* * * * * * * * * * * * * * * *

Helen Fairchild Smith, dean of Wells College

across the room from Dean Smith was all that was needed to let a student know her legs weren't properly crossed or her dress was too casual for the occasion. Dean Smith also stressed the importance of academics—literature, science, and the arts above all. One's studies, however, were to complement, not compete with, proper social training.

Frances's popularity with young men certainly did not abate while she attended an all-women's college. On one day in 1882, she received two

Frances Folsom (second from left, back row) poses with classmates at Wells College.

Grover Cleveland as governor of New York

marriage proposals at once, both from sons of prominent New York families. Very shortly afterward, she was visited by her mother, Emma Folsom, who seemed to question whether Frances could manage such a busy social life and her college studies at the same time. She reminded Frances to view college as a once-in-a-lifetime opportunity, something not to be wasted.

In 1883, Grover Cleveland was elected governor of New York. Emma and Frank paid a visit to the Executive Mansion in Albany soon after he took

Frances and her mother visited Grover at the Governor's Mansion in Albany not long after he moved in.

31

The State Capitol in Albany, New York, as it looked when Grover Cleveland was governor

A view of Albany in 1878

up residence. During the visit, both Frances and the governor were aware that their feelings for each other had changed. One of Cleveland's aides at the time remembered the governor saying, "If one of you young fellows doesn't take an interest in the pretty Miss Folsom, the governor is likely to walk off with her himself!"

For her part, Frances was flattered by the governor's attention. When he wrote to her at Wells, she answered immediately. He began sending flowers and candy, often every week. As the letters between the two became more frequent and more tender, Grover felt obliged to write to Emma Folsom, asking permission to court her daughter. Emma didn't object, especially since she knew of Frank's growing love for Grover.

Frank had, in fact, spilled her heart

Ever Faithfully Yours

✴ ✴

Not surprisingly, Grover and Frances carried on much of their courtship through the U.S. mail since they lived apart. This was not entirely a function of geography, however. In the infancy of the telephone and well before e-mail, letter writing achieved the status of a high art. Victorians were expert letter writers and spent a good deal of time corresponding with friends and relatives. And the handwritten letter was perfect for expressing intimate feelings in a society that discouraged outright demonstrations of affection. The love letter was considered the prelude to marriage and was to be written with the "utmost regard for perfection." It was up to the man to begin the correspondence with a lady, bravely risking rejection. In its chapter on "Letters of Love," one etiquette book of the period advises: "Of all letters, the love-letter should be the most carefully prepared. They are the most thoroughly read and re-read, the longest preserved, and the most likely to be regretted in after life." Whether or not he had read such advice, Grover's very proper love letters evidently had their desired effect.

Frances Folsom in 1885, the year Grover Cleveland became president of the United States

him!" Emma advised her daughter not to worry, that after all the governor had political battles to fight—and, oh, yes, there's talk that the Democrats might nominate him for the presidency in 1884.

Grover Cleveland's rise to national prominence seemed to come very quickly, but, in fact, as soon as he was elected governor of New York, he was talked about as a possible presidential candidate. New York was not only the most populous state in the Union in 1884, its political "machines" were the most powerful as well. The fact that Cleveland had the muscle and clout to win the gubernatorial election meant that he was already a contender for the presidency.

The governor was hard at work at his desk in Albany when he received the news from the Democratic Convention in Chicago that he'd been nominated on the second ballot. Cannons could be heard exploding in the distance, and an aide reportedly rushed in exclaiming, "They are firing a salute, Governor, for your nomination!" Governor Cleveland looked at the man thoughtfully, "Do you think

out to her mother, telling her how she wished Grover could spend more time with her . . . and less governing the state of New York!

"He certainly is a funny man," Frank wrote. "I can't quite fathom

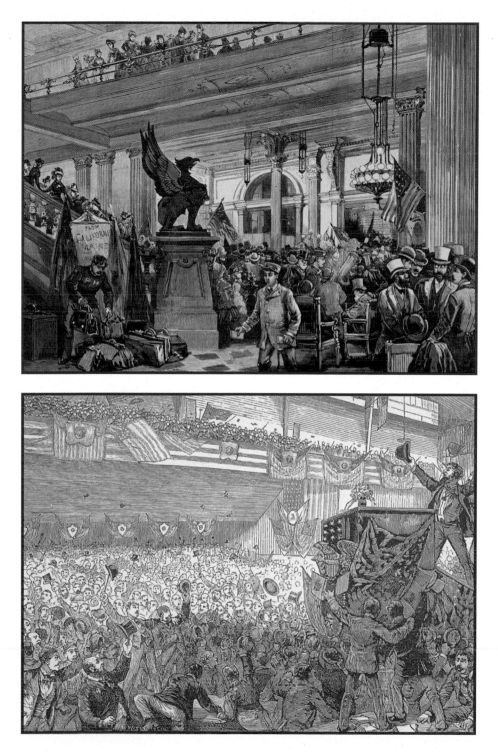

The 1884 Democratic National Convention was held in Chicago's Palmer House hotel (left).

Delegates to the convention raise their hats and cheer at the announcement of Cleveland's nomination as the Democratic candidate for president.

Convention delegates and excited Chicagoans formed a torchlight parade outside the Palmer House in honor of Cleveland's nomination.

James G. Blaine, Republican candidate for president

Buffalo welcomed candidate Cleveland with fireworks and a huge parade.

This pro-Cleveland political cartoon shows the Democrat telling the truth about his personal life while Republican Blaine tries to conceal his sins.

Voters discuss the presidential candidates.

so?" he said. "Well, anyhow we'll need to finish up this work."

A very arduous campaign followed Grover Cleveland's nomination. His opponent, Republican James Blaine of Maine, fought hard, using every weapon at his disposal. Blaine's staff members visited Buffalo and interviewed as many of Grover Cleveland's former political enemies as they could. They worked with eager reporters to bring to the surface old rumors about the governor's private life. Wasn't it true, they asked, that back in the old days, when Cleveland frequented Buffalo's saloons, he knew a woman named Maria Halpin—a woman of very questionable morals? And that Maria later gave birth to a son who was now about ten years old? Was it even possible that Cleveland himself was the father? Grover Cleveland confounded his critics by answering honestly that, yes, he'd supported both Maria Halpin and her son for many years, though he'd never considered marrying Mrs. Halpin.

In the end, Grover Cleveland connected with voters by promising to clean up government. His belief, stat-

Well-Oiled Machines

✯ ✯

With the explosive growth of cities in the later nineteenth century, a crop of corrupt, but powerful political machines also sprouted. Run by greedy city leaders called bosses, they traded votes for city services, contracts for kickbacks, and jobs for loyalty. Whatever their methods, the machines got things done and eased the urban growing pains of Chicago, Philadelphia, Boston, San Francisco, and other American cities. The most powerful machine of the period was New York City's Tammany Hall. Tammany was an Indian name adopted by a fraternity of Revolutionary War soldiers in 1789. Over the years, Tammany developed into the New York Democratic party organization, sinking to its lowest level under William Marcy Tweed after 1851. Serving in nearly every city and state post over the next twenty years, colorful "Boss" Tweed led a conspiracy of corruption that

A Nast cartoon showing a corrupt Boss Tweed

bilked the city out of tens of millions of dollars. Consider this scam: It should have cost $250,000 to build the New York County Courthouse. By the time the Tweed Ring was through lining its pockets, the bill exceeded $13 million. Through the work of honest politicians and an outraged press, Tweed's generation of Tammany Hall collapsed in 1871. The machine endured well into the twentieth century, however, under the leadership of other bosses.

ed often, that "Public office is a public trust," distinguished him from other politicians of the day, who fully intended to use their elected positions for their own benefit. Another slogan, "You'll love him for the enemies he's made!" referred to public corruption in general, but to Tammany Hall in particular. The bosses of Tammany Hall—a symbol of political power in New York City for several generations—were particularly skillful at manipulating government money and jobs.

When Grover Cleveland became the twenty-second president of the United States on March 4, 1885, no one was more surprised than he himself. "It is as if fate and destiny formed a partnership," he wrote to a friend, ". . . I have done so little to merit so awesome a responsibility." Indeed, there was to be no break from the pressure of the campaign, no allowance for learning on the job. As usual,

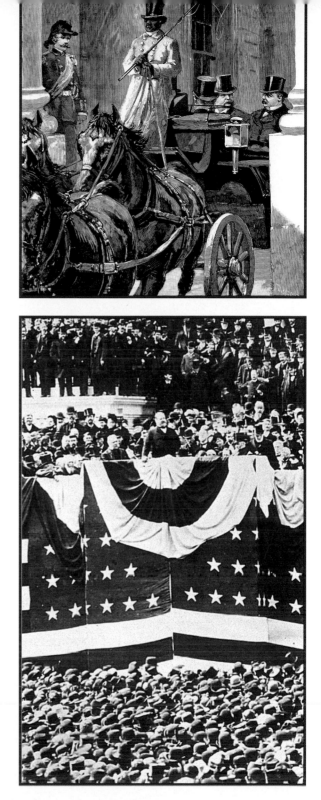

Top: President Chester Arthur and President-elect Grover Cleveland on their way to Cleveland's inauguration

Right: Cleveland delivering his inauguration speech

39

The capstone was placed on the Washington Monument on December 6, 1884.

When Frank visited Grover in Washington, D.C., she was impressed by the new monument.

he set to his various tasks with a tremendous appetite for work.

Rose Cleveland, the youngest of Grover's eight brothers and sisters, became the official White House hostess. She cheerfully presided over state dinners and receptions. Washington society, however, found her a bit odd; at least she wasn't what they were used to. Rose, known as Lizzie, was very well educated and extremely opinionated. She did not enjoy small talk. She once

Pennsylvania Avenue, Washington, D.C., as viewed from the Treasury Building in 1885. The Capitol can be seen at the end of the street.

Hostess with the Mostess

✶ ✶

Although the role of White House hostess has diminished in importance in the twentieth century, it was at one time a crucial job. After all, a successful dinner party or an elegant reception brought important people together and might help make some friends for the president. A hostess with good social skills could greatly influence the reputation of the administration. In most cases, the First Lady served as White House hostess. Martha Washington began the 140-year tradition of opening the president's home to all visitors on New Year's Day, but it was the vivacious Dolley Madison, wife of the fourth president, who truly defined the social role of the First Lady as hostess. She loved entertaining, and often served ice cream to her startled guests. In the 1870s, Julia Grant entertained extravagantly, sometimes serving up to twenty-one dinner courses. And Frances Cleveland's receptions were so popular that she once had to have her arm massaged before she could continue shaking hands with her 8,000 guests. For various reasons, thirteen presidents have asked family members or friends to serve as White House hostesses. His wife deceased, Thomas Jefferson engaged Dolley Madison, whose husband was then secretary of state. Several other First Ladies were too ill to serve, and Jane Appleton Pierce was too deep in grief over the death of her young son to socialize. Grover Cleveland's sister Rose served until he married, leaving James Buchanan the only bachelor to require a hostess—his niece—because he never married.

Rose Cleveland

admitted that while standing for a long time in a White House receiving line, she overcame her boredom by silently conjugating Greek verbs.

There were many who believed Grover Cleveland would likely remain a bachelor, if not his whole life, at least during his presidency. He was not particularly handsome and was quite overweight. Still, many women in Washington society were intrigued by the prospect of marrying a president and asked to be introduced. His reply, however, was inevitably, "Too busy!" When one of his sisters asked him whether he'd ever marry, he answered that he'd thought about marriage a good many times and "the more I think about it, the more I'll not do it."

The truth was, however, that shortly after taking office, he'd made the decision to propose to Frances Folsom. In March 1885, he welcomed Frank and Emma to the White House. It was Frank's spring break from Wells College, and it was her first visit to Washington. "I can't begin to tell how it all impressed me as we drove up to the house, catching on the way a glimpse of the Capitol, the Treasury,

the Monument. . . ." There were many late-night walks through the house with Grover, and it is believed that at some point during the visit they discussed the possibility of marriage.

Frank returned to Wells College and graduated in June. In August, while on vacation in the Adirondacks, she received a letter from Grover proposing marriage. He asked her to consider the matter carefully, to be "selfish" in making her decision. He men-

Frank received Grover's letter proposing marriage while she was vacationing in the Adirondacks.

Frank enjoyed beautiful sunsets like this one during her vacation in the Adirondack Mountains.

tioned that he hoped her love for him was true and not just a substitute for the love of her father. Frank wrote back immediately, saying she had loved him for a very long time. Members of both families were told of the engagement and everyone agreed to keep the secret until the official announcement was made.

In October, Frank, Emma, and Frank's cousin Ben Folsom, set sail for England. A brief article in the *New York World* noted her departure under the heading, "Miss Folsom Going Abroad." Indeed, rumors of her involvement with the president were already in wide circulation.

Grover wanted, above all else, to protect Frank from overzealous reporters and Washington gossipmon-

gers. He heartily approved of the plan to send Frances to Europe with her mother; he wanted them out of harm's way as marriage speculation grew. While the two women shopped for the wedding trousseau in London and Paris and visited museums throughout England, France, Italy, Germany, Austria, and Belgium, the American press went to work.

Only in April, while Frances and her mother were touring Europe, did speculation about the president's wedding plans spill onto the front pages of the country's newspapers. "WASHINGTON GOSSIP!" blared a headline of the *New York Herald* on April 19, 1886. "Society Incredulous about the President's Marriage—What If It Proves True?"

There was just one more detail reporters needed before breaking the story wide open: Which of the two Folsom women was to be the bride— Frances or her mother, Emma? Most "experts" picked Emma, the widow of Cleveland's law partner, Oscar Folsom. Hadn't she, after all, relied on Grover for both legal and personal advice since her husband's accidental death nearly ten years before? And wasn't Frances, twenty-seven years younger than the president, just a bit too young?

Articles were written about the suitability of the president marrying such a young girl. Better, many editorials suggested, to marry the mother than the daughter. Newspapers were not alone in hinting that the marriage was less than desirable. Frank's own school friend, Kate Willard, responded to the news by asking her to reconsider: "You are so young and sweet and I have always thought you would love someone younger. . . ."

The press interviewed anyone who might have any insight as to the bride's identity. A former Cleveland aide claimed that several years ago, he'd overheard the then-governor say he was "waiting for my wife to grow up." Another insider observed the president fuming over why "the papers keep marrying me to old ladies. . . ." As April turned to May, everyone began to agree that Miss Frances Folsom was to be the president's bride.

On May 15, Frances, Emma, and Ben boarded the steamer *Noordland* in Antwerp, Belgium, and began the long journey to New York. Secrecy was the order of the day. The plan was so complete, in fact, that luggage stenciled with the initials "F.C.F." was sent to Liverpool, England, and placed on another ship. Reporters noted in both European and American papers that the "president's bride," who had previously been believed to be sailing from Antwerp was, in fact, leaving from Liverpool.

Frank wasn't a bit surprised to find her stateroom aboard the *Noordland* filled with flowers from Grover. She filled her last days of anonymity on board the ship reading and relaxing. She also wrote a short story about a homeless girl who peddled newspapers on the streets of New York City

The Folsoms sent initialed luggage to Liverpool, England (left), so reporters would not know that Emma and Frances were really leaving Europe on a ship that was sailing from Antwerp, Belgium.

until she met and married a wealthy older man.

On May 26, a pilot boat was dispatched from New York Harbor to meet the *Noordland*. Just before the steamer's entrance to the harbor, passengers gathered at the rail to watch the Folsom party leave the ship for the small boat. Word spread quickly that this indeed was the woman who would become the next First Lady. The ship's passengers waved their hats and handkerchiefs while the ship's captain "grasped the cord of the whistle and blew a blast that would have put the sounds of wedding bells quite in the shade."

When the *Noordland* arrived at its dock, the gangplank was mobbed by reporters. But where was Miss Folsom?

The ship's passengers and crew seemed to delight in telling about the bride-to-be's "daring" escape. Much to the press's dismay, Frances was now safely secluded in her New York hotel room!

The next day, May 28, the president met with his cabinet and gave each member an invitation written in his own hand: *On Wednesday next at seven o'clock in the evening I shall be married to Miss Folsom at the White House. We shall have a very quiet wedding, but I earnestly desire that you be present at that occasion.*

He then excused himself and made the public announcement, confirming what everyone had suspected for weeks. The only surprise was that the wedding was to take place in only five days!

CHAPTER FOUR

A National Obsession

Once the official engagement announcement was made, the country was in the grips of "Frankie mania." Everyone, it seemed, wanted to catch a glimpse of Frances Folsom's beautiful dark eyes, wavy chestnut-colored hair, and lovely warm smile. During her stay in New York City, any possible "Frankie sightings" turned entire city blocks into scenes of confusion.

The speed of her fame was breathtaking. Within a week, it seemed, her hairstyle—a simple knot at the back of her head—had become all the rage. Women across the country lined up to have their pictures taken with just the expression and tilt of the head Frankie

Worth a Thousand Words

★ ★

The national celebrity status that Frances Cleveland achieved was unusual, especially for a woman, at that time. Improvements in photography and picture making fueled her popularity, while an eager national press distributed her image around the country. So admired was her portrait that women flocked to have their pictures taken, tilting their heads just so in imitation of Frankie. Her picture decorated people's homes, joining framed friends and relatives on crowded mantelpieces. Smiling from campaign posters in 1888 and 1892, Frances unwittingly launched a new election tactic: running for First Lady. Everyone wanted a piece of Frankie's popularity and beauty. Without asking, manufacturers of everything from thread to soaps plastered her likeness all over their advertisements. Finally, in 1888 Congress introduced a bill to prohibit the use of the image of "any female living or dead, who is or was the wife, mother, daughter or sister of any citizen of the United States" without their consent. The bill didn't pass. Those early advertisers were onto something: a popular picture sells products. Today, pictures of celebrity endorsers are worth far more than a thousand words.

favored. In fact, thousands of Frankie photographs were sold and displayed proudly in homes throughout the country.

President Cleveland traveled to New York City both to greet Frank and to preside over the annual Memorial Day parade, which he would watch from a reviewing stand on Fifth Avenue. The atmosphere was festive, to say the least. Crowds laughed as many of the marching

New York City's Wall Street in the 1880s

A traffic jam on Broadway at the time President Cleveland was in New York to greet Frank

Well-dressed New Yorkers take a Saturday afternoon stroll on Broadway at Madison Square.

49

President Cleveland presided over the 1886 New York City Memorial Day parade, which marched down Broadway, shown here on a quieter day.

Frances watched the parade from a window of the Fifth Avenue Hotel (below), which overlooked the reviewing stand.

bands played popular tunes such as "Come to Where My Love Lies Dreaming" and "He's Going to Marry Yum-Yum!" from Gilbert and Sullivan's *The Mikado*. They even broke into "The Wedding March."

Frank watched the parade from a window of the Fifth Avenue Hotel, which overlooked the reviewing stand. From the hotel, Frank could see the back of Grover's head. At one point, someone passed a message to the president that his fiancée was watching from a nearby window. He turned from the parade and raised his hat to her. She replied by smiling and

A Smash Hit

☆ ☆

The Mikado was an enormously successful comic operetta written by the darlings of London musical theater, William Gilbert and Arthur Sullivan. Gilbert and Sullivan are also famous for *H.M.S. Pinafore, The Pirates of Penzance,* and many other light operas. Their style, which combined popular music, romance, and humor, evolved over the years into the musicals that Broadway loves today. *The Mikado* had opened in London the year before Frances's wedding to Grover. It relates the comic love story between Nanki-Poo, son of the Mikado (emperor), and the beautiful Yum-Yum in a Japanese village called Titipu. The fanciful Japanese setting undoubtedly pleased theatergoers at the time. Trading between the United States and Japan had begun in earnest in 1853, and in the years that followed, Japanese art and culture greatly influenced western fashion, painting, architecture, and home furnishings.

HOLLIS STREET THEATRE

PROPRIETOR AND MANAGER, MR. ISAAC B. RICH.
ASSISTANT MANAGER, MR. CHARLES J. RICH.

GALA NIGHT.

Monday Evening, January 18th, 1886.

80TH

PERFORMANCE OF

GILBERT AND SULLIVAN'S

JAPANESE OPERA, IN TWO ACTS.

THE MIKADO,

OR THE "TOWN OF TITIPU,"

PRESENTED BY

D'OYLY CARTE'S OPERA COMPANY.

Under the Management of Mr. JOHN STETSON.

Dramatis Personæ.

THE MIKADO of JAPAN.
MR. E. S. GRANT.

NANKI-POO, . . his son, in love with Yum-Yum,
MR. L. CADWALLADR.

KO-KO, ... Lord High Executioner,
MR. RICHARD MANSFIELD.

POOH-BAH, . . . Lord High Everything Else,
SIG. BROCOLINI.

PISH-TUSH, ... a Noble Lord.
MR. GEORGE OLMI.

YUM-YUM,
MISS IDA MÜLLE.

PITTI-SING,
MISS HATTIE DELARO.

PEEP-BO,
MISS EDITH JENNESSE.
(Three Sisters, Wards of Ko-Ko.)

KATISHA, ... in love with Nanki-Poo.
MISS ROSA COOKE.

MR. STETSON'S STAFF.
MUSICAL DIRECTOR—Mr. JOHN BRAHAM.
BUSINESS MANAGER—Mr. FRANK PILLING.
STAGE MANAGER—Mr. F. A. LEON.

A Puck cartoon congratulating Grover Cleveland on his marriage to Frances Folsom

waving her lace handkerchief. The crowd cheered wildly.

Frank and Emma remained in New York until June 1, when they boarded a train for Washington, D.C. They arrived very early in the morning on June 2 and were whisked to the White House, arriving just ahead of dozens of reporters. Inside the mansion, Grover joined mother and daughter for breakfast before returning to presidential business.

The beautiful satin wedding dress that Frances wore is displayed at the Smithsonian Institution.

Frances and her mother embrace after the marriage vows had been spoken.

By seven o'clock, Frances had become a fairy-tale bride. The guests gasped when they saw the lace veil framing her face and the dreamy white train that trailed down the grand staircase. Frances and Grover were married by Grover's Presbyterian minister, Byron Sutherland. After handshakes, hugs, and kisses, the happy wedding party and guests headed into the State Dining Room for an informal supper. Letters and telegrams of congratulation were read, including one from Queen Victoria.

By nine o'clock, the newlyweds were in their traveling clothes, heading into a carriage that would take them to the train station. The crowd outside, expecting the festivities to last longer, missed the departure. It wasn't until they heard the sound of the carriage on the street that they realized the new Mr. and Mrs. Cleveland had already left the White House.

Unfortunately, privacy was not so easily achieved during the Clevelands' honeymoon. The location, Deer Park in western Maryland, had been chosen for its remoteness. But by the time they arrived at the honeymoon cottage in the early morning of June 3, the press had already set up its observation sites.

Communication lines to various national newspapers were in place, ready to monitor the couple's every step outside the cottage. This form of

Frances, who was an immediate success as a hostess, is shown here greeting guests at a formal White House reception in honor of officers of the army and navy.

"keyhole journalism," as it came to be known, included going through the day's trash and the dirty laundry, as well as waylaying waiters and chambermaids on their way to and from the cottage and the main lodge.

As soon as the honeymoon was over, Frances assumed her duties as First Lady with enthusiasm and charm. Her success as a hostess was immediate—a tribute, she often claimed, to the rigorous training of Dean Smith at Wells College. She seemed completely at ease during the afternoon receptions, which required her to stand for hours, shaking hands, smiling, and exchanging niceties.

Though Frank stayed out of the political arena, she did ruffle some feathers when she began holding public receptions on Saturday afternoons. The reason for such a time change, she made clear, was so that working women could visit the White House. When she was soundly criticized for encouraging "a great rabble of shop-

Women at Work

✯ ✯

By the time Frances became First Lady, industry had revolutionized America. Products once homemade could now be mass-produced. New inventions—from the telephone to the safety pin—needed to be made and operated or sold by somebody. Cities and industrial centers thrived, and, although most Americans still lived in rural areas, many came to the cities to seek their fortunes. Immigrants from Europe and Asia flocked to share in the bonanza.

And women joined the throng. Between 1865 and 1890, the number of women wage earners in the United States tripled. Many were young and single, beginning to work around age fifteen and quitting at marriage in their early twenties. Indeed, by 1900, only 5 percent of all married women worked outside the home. In African-American families, however, 25 percent of wives were employed.

The jobs available to women were limited. While industry had created unheard-of opportunities and products, it had also made some Americans very wealthy. The gap between rich and poor, especially in the cities, grew broader and broader. As a result, most working women found jobs as cooks, laundresses, and servants to America's wealthy families. Many of the rest worked in textile and garment factories. Their wages ranged from an average of $4 per week to $6.90, about half of what men earned. They worked long hours, often ten hours a day six days a week. No wonder the rich got richer! As clerical work expanded, women called "typewriters" learned new skills such as typing and stenography and sought office jobs. Among the professions, a few college-educated women became lawyers and doctors. Most turned to teaching or nursing.

Frances championed the industrious "shopgirls" and other working women of her era in an early attempt to recognize the hard work that women contributed to the American economy.

President Grover Cleveland and First Lady Frances often entertained visiting dignitaries at formal White House State Dinners.

To escape the pressures of living full-time at the White House, Frances and Grover spent much of every fall and spring at Oak View, their suburban home.

The Clevelands spent summers at Gray Gables, their home in Buzzards Bay, Massachusetts.

girls" to mill about the mansion, she refused to budge. Because of such boldness, Frances became even more popular with middle-class women.

Frances Folsom Cleveland later attributed her relaxed social manner to the fact that she spent less time living at the White House than any First Lady before or since. The Clevelands actually bought a home for themselves in the suburbs of Washington—just a 3-mile (5-km) drive from the White House—and they lived there for most of every fall and spring. It was only during the winter—at the height of the social season—that they were full-time residents of the White House. In the summer, the Clevelands left the Washington area completely, moving to their home in Buzzards Bay, Massachusetts.

As the First Lady's popularity continued to grow, the president's numerous political enemies became nervous. The Republicans, in particular, were hoping they could run a strong campaign in 1888 and block Cleveland's reelection. After the president's mar-

The Capitol as it looked in 1886

This photograph of Frances was taken in 1886.

riage, however, they knew they would need to counter the favorable publicity enjoyed by his bride.

The president often seemed to help his enemies with very public outbursts against the press. Once during a speech, when he verbally attacked a group of reporters and photographers who paid more attention to the First Lady than to him, the press countered by accusing him of being jealous. That seemed to lead the press—prodded by the president's political enemies—to search for signs of disharmony in the marriage. As the election of 1888 drew near, stories began to appear that undercut the couple's image as happily married. Frances was reportedly seen, for example, riding in a carriage with an unmarried gentleman.

Finally, when a so-called exposé appeared that claimed to have seen Frances running from the White House after the president had beaten her, she decided it was time to answer the charges. Mrs. Cleveland had almost never spoken directly to the press, so her candor in itself was newsworthy. Her comments, released for publication, were in the form of a let-

First Lady Frances Folsom Cleveland is shown in her White House sitting room about 1887.

Frances Cleveland spends a quiet moment at the beautiful lunette window in the West Hall of the White House.

ter to another woman who had written asking to know the truth about the Cleveland marriage. This woman's minister had delivered a sermon harshly criticizing the president's treatment of his wife.

Frances responded by calling the charges "wicked and heartless lies." "I can only wish the women of our country," she continued, "no better blessing than that their homes and their lives may be as happy and that their husbands may be as kind and affectionate as mine."

Some Democratic party members, eager to use Mrs. Cleveland's tremendous popularity, had campaign posters made with her picture in between those of the president and his running mate, Allen G. Thurman. The Clevelands, as always, did not give their approval to such a use of Frances's picture.

This campaign, unlike the last one, was more about political substance than character. The great issue of the day was the tariff. The Republicans wanted to protect high tariffs on American goods and, in effect,

Benjamin Harrison in his office receiving election returns that would confirm his election as president

squelch free trade among nations. President Cleveland preferred that tariffs be lowered to promote competition and help the economy.

In a disappointing loss for both Grover and Frances, Benjamin Harrison was elected to become the twenty-third president. The Clevelands, however, were certain they wouldn't be away long. Grover wasn't even fifty yet and had every intention of run-

Before leaving the White House, the Clevelands entertained President-elect Benjamin Harrison and his family at a welcoming dinner.

ning again in four years. Frances, if anything, was even more confident that she'd live in the White House again one day. "Now, Jerry," she told one of the trusted White House servants as she was leaving, "I want you to take good care of all the furniture and ornaments in the house, for I want to find everything just as it is now when we come back again four years from today."

And come back she would.

☆　☆　☆　☆　☆　☆　☆　☆　☆　☆　☆　☆　☆　☆

CHAPTER FIVE

Panic

☆ ☆ ☆ ☆ ☆ ☆ ☆ ☆ ☆ ☆ ☆ ☆ ☆ ☆ ☆ ☆

Mr. and Mrs. Grover Cleveland tried to return to as private a life as they could, considering they had just moved from the White House. They decided to move to New York City, where the former president joined a corporate law firm. Grover was able to live a life he'd never had before. He went to his office each morning, worked until late in the afternoon, walked home or to his club, and enjoyed time with family and friends. The Clevelands, for the moment, were out of the limelight, and they seemed to love it. They were both later to describe the four years between the two presidential terms as the happiest of their marriage.

☆ ☆ ☆ ☆ ☆ ☆ ☆ ☆ ☆ ☆ ☆ ☆ ☆ ☆ ☆ ☆

Frances with the Clevelands' first child, affectionately referred to as "Baby Ruth"

When their first child, Ruth, was born in 1891, Frank and Grover were overjoyed. The new father, who was fifty-four, wrote to a friend that it seemed as though he'd just entered the real world, where he could "see in a small child more value than I have ever called my own before." Just as marriage softened the hard edges of the tough politician, so fatherhood mellowed Grover Cleveland further.

By the time of Ruth's birth, however-er, the presidential election of 1892 was already looming. Despite Grover Cleveland's popularity among Eastern Democrats, he was not certain of winning the party's nomination. The country was changing quickly, growing larger and more diverse. Labor unions were forming and engaging in dramatic struggles with big business.

Steelworkers in Homestead, Pennsylvania, staged a violent strike in 1892.

This political cartoon during the presidential campaign of 1892 shows President Cleveland running for reelection on the back of his popular wife.

Midwestern farmers and western ranchers were also making demands that clashed with the desires of Easterners.

There were also signs of serious economic problems that would plague either candidate. The voters were in a serious, even ominous, mood. The Democrats turned to Grover Cleveland when they sensed that no one else would have a chance of beating the incumbent, President Benjamin Harrison.

The Clevelands were at their summer home in Buzzards Bay, Massachusetts, on Election Day 1892. Grover had spent several hours at his favorite pastime, fishing. That evening, as his family and friends tallied the results and tried to predict the out-

President Cleveland giving his second Inauguration speech.

This Inauguration badge was issued by Tammany Hall to celebrate Cleveland's return to the White House in 1893.

come, he announced, "I forgot to dry my lines today." He calmly left the gathering to go back outside to hang his fishing lines. When he returned to the house, he was greeted with the news that he'd been reelected to the presidency.

By Inauguration Day in 1893, Grover Cleveland knew the country was on the brink of financial collapse. Factories and railroads were going bankrupt; banks were failing; stock prices on Wall Street were in a free fall. And, worst of all, gold reserves in the Treasury were at their lowest levels ever. Cleveland placed most of the blame for this situation on the Sherman Silver Purchase Act, which he vowed to repeal. (This law, backed by Western silver interests, allowed for the minting of a greater number of silver coins. When the price of silver fell as a result, a run on Treasury reserves of gold followed. This threatened the stability of the national Treasury.)

President Grover Cleveland and former President Benjamin Harrison returning to the White House from the Inauguration

As stock prices continued to fall during Cleveland's second term, Wall Street traders (below) rushed to sell stocks for their clients.

The president called for a special session of Congress in August to settle this matter. He knew he would need all his strength to force a reluctant Congress to repeal the law. In June 1893, however, a malignant tumor was found in Cleveland's jaw, and his doctors insisted he have immediate surgery to remove it. The president and his closest advisers believed, however, that the country's economic health was too fragile to risk letting the public know about the life-or-death operation. They insisted on complete secrecy.

Chicago's Great White City

✴ ✴

A ticket to the Columbian Exposition

The Ferris Wheel

All eyes turned to Chicago on May 1, 1893, for the opening of the dazzling World's Columbian Exposition. This was to be the greatest world's fair ever, held on 550 acres (223 hectares) along Chicago's lakefront. The grandeur of its gleaming white buildings gave it the name "White City." More than a million objects celebrated the world's progress in science, industry, and art since the voyage of Christopher Columbus 500 years before. At precisely 12:08 A.M. on opening day, President Cleveland pressed the master switch to electrify lights, fountains, and machinery. Never before had people witnessed such an awesome display of electricity, that mysterious new invisible power source. Besides electricity, all the wonders of the modern world thrilled the 21 million visitors who flocked to the fair that summer. Moving pictures, refrigeration, fine art, a ten-ton cheese, and the world's first hot dogs delighted fairgoers. For pleasure-minded visitors, sideshows lined the Midway. Exotic replicas of faraway places included the "Streets of Cairo" pavilion. There the famous belly dancer "Little Egypt" did the "hootchy-kootchy," distressing the proper ladies in the crowd. Most spectacular of all, the 250-foot (76-m) Ferris wheel towered above the grounds. An engineering marvel, the wheel symbolized both the fun and the wonder of the World's Columbian Exposition.

Left: The Art Palace at night

Bottom left: "The Watergate"

Below: The Administration Building

nation being the president's summer home on Cape Cod.

On the afternoon of June 30, President Cleveland and his secretary of war, Daniel Lamont, boarded a train in Washington for New York City. That same day, the *Oneida* was transformed into a floating hospital, complete with operating table and all the

Cleveland's jaw surgery was performed aboard the yacht Oneida, *owned by Commodore Benedict.*

Frances Cleveland (center) posed with wives of the president's cabinet members in 1894.

But how? The president asked for the help of his good friend, Commodore Benedict, who owned a large luxury yacht. After much consultation, it was agreed that the surgery would take place on board the *Oneida* as it moved slowly up New York's East River and then out to the Atlantic Ocean. The cruise would have all the outward appearances of a relaxing outing with a friend, with the final desti-

A Presidential Coincidence

☆ ☆

Grover Cleveland's mouth had been painful for several weeks before doctors determined that the cigar-smoking president suffered from a cancerous lesion there. Cleveland and his advisers were well aware of the grave possibilities; former president Ulysses S. Grant, who also loved his cigars, had died in 1884 from cancer of the throat. The plan they devised, involving delicate surgery on a sailing vessel, posed some obvious problems. But, on blessedly quiet seas, five eminent doctors and a New York dentist—an expert in a new anesthesia called nitrous oxide, or "laughing gas"—made the two-hour operation a success. Twenty-seven years later, Dr. William W. Keen, one of those physicians, published a book that revealed the entire story for the first time. In 1921, that same Dr. Keen, by then eighty-four, attended a rising young politician named Franklin Roosevelt who had lost all movement in his legs. Keen diagnosed a temporary condition and charged the Roosevelts $600. He could not have been more wrong. The future thirty-second president suffered the rest of his life from crippling polio.

necessary medical supplies. When President Cleveland and Secretary Lamont arrived very late that night, five doctors on board were ready to begin surgery.

As the anesthesia was administered to the president, the *Oneida* slowly left its mooring. Belowdecks, the head surgeon began cutting through the president's upper left jawbone, scraping away all the cancerous matter. When the operation was over, the doctor closed the wound and packed Cleveland's mouth with gauze. Word was sent to Frances in Buzzards Bay that all was well.

Two days later, on July 3, the patient was up and walking on the deck. Just as scheduled, on July 5, the *Oneida* arrived in Buzzards Bay. President Cleveland, wrapped in a cloak, left the yacht and walked unaided up the dock and into his home, Gray Gables.

Reporters, stationed outside the president's home during his vacation, were told the president had merely had two teeth pulled. At the end of August, a Philadelphia newspaper ran the story of the president's secret surgery. No one, however, could verify the details and the information was considered too far-fetched to be believable. The truth about the president's secret operation wasn't completely disclosed until twenty-five years later.

While the president struggled with the nation's economy and his own health, his family thrived. Frances, it was noted by the newspapers, had matured from a young bride into a lovely mother. Much attention was focused, of course, on their infant daughter, Ruth, who quickly became the darling of the entire nation. Why, a new candy bar was even named for her—Baby Ruth!

In September 1893, Frances Cleve-

Frances with Ruth (left) and Esther

land gave birth to Esther, the only child of a president ever born in the White House. The president's two young daughters provided him great relief during a period of nearly constant economic, social, and political crises. ". . . I often think," he wrote to a friend, "that if things should go wrong at that end of the house, I should abandon the ship!"

At times, it must have seemed to the beleaguered president that he

Frances the First

★ ★

First Lady Frances Folsom Cleveland caused quite a stir. As the youngest presidential wife and certainly the first to enjoy such popularity, Frances has become associated with a long list of White House firsts. She was the first presidential bride to be married in the executive mansion, and, later, the first presidential widow to remarry. Because of her overwhelming popularity, Frances was the first First Lady to require a professional assistant. The first remark ever about a First Lady at a convention was made in 1888—to riotous applause. Frances was the one and only First Lady to return to the White House after a one-term absence. Her daughter Esther was the first child born in the White House. Indeed, like lives of modern celebrities, Frances's life in the public eye brought both rewards and difficulties.

Frances Folsom Cleveland

couldn't do anything right. Despite his success in overturning the Sherman Silver Purchase Act, the nation's economic depression continued. Western farmers revolted over low crop prices, and midwestern and eastern workers staged costly labor strikes.

In 1894, a long strike by railroad workers at Chicago's Pullman Company threatened to spin out of control. When word reached Washington that strikers were preventing train cars loaded with U.S. mail from leaving the city, President Cleveland decided

*During the Pullman
Company railroad
strike, rioters
wrecked an engine
and freight cars.*

*National Guardsmen fire at the strikers to try to
gain control of the trains.*

*The first meat train leaves the Chicago stockyards
under escort of the United States Cavalry.*

74

Eugene V. Debs, president of the American Railway Union

it was time to intervene. The Pullman Company owners asked for federal troops to break up the strike, and the president agreed. Workers across the country were outraged: they believed that Cleveland had taken the owners' word over that of the American Railway Union leader, Eugene V. Debs. In their view, Cleveland could never again call himself a friend of working men and women.

Frances Cleveland hated reading all the criticism written about her husband. Eventually, as his popularity

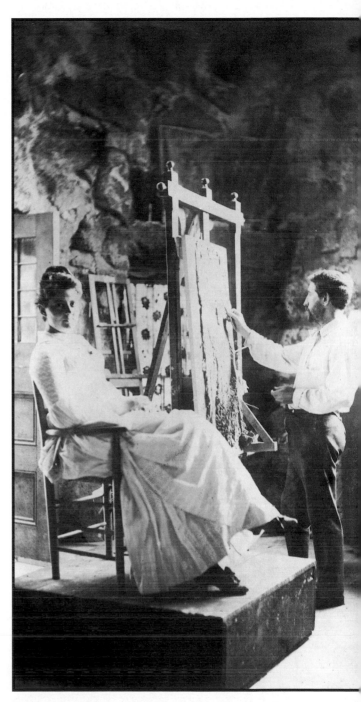

Frances posed for artist Augustus St. Gaudens in his studio, 1894.

plummeted, so did hers. Even Ruth and Esther weren't spared the harsh glare of the media spotlight. When the toddlers weren't seen in public for several weeks, reporters asked if they were developing normally. What exactly, they wanted to know were the Clevelands trying to hide?

As discouraged as Frances was by the press's mean-spiritedness, she vowed to continue greeting the public at White House receptions. The Clevelands had given up private entertaining during this economic depression. Frances, however, felt it her duty to shake hands and exchange pleasant words with visitors several times a week.

By 1896, Grover Cleveland, worn out by the trials of his second term, decided not to seek reelection. Although the Democratic party was

William Jennings Bryan was the Democratic candidate for president in 1896.

This political cartoon shows McKinley defending his country when Bryan was still only a baby.

deeply divided over who should lead it, members were united in blaming the president for the nation's problems. He could now only watch from the sidelines as the party nominated William Jennings Bryan for the presidency.

Bryan was defeated in 1896 by Republican William McKinley. As soon as McKinley was sworn into office, a disheartened Grover Cleveland left Washington and politics forever. He told a close a friend at the time that he believed himself to be the most unpopular person in the entire country.

Medals and buttons like these were worn by supporters of Republican William McKinley during the 1896 election campaign.

President McKinley at his desk in 1898

77

CHAPTER SIX

A New Life, Again

✫ ✫ ✫ ✫ ✫ ✫ ✫ ✫ ✫ ✫ ✫ ✫ ✫ ✫ ✫ ✫

When the date of Mrs. Cleveland's last Saturday reception for working women was announced, the public finally seemed to realize this would be their last chance to meet "Frankie." Many visitors arrived at the White House before dawn to assure a place in line. When the doors opened, more than 23,000 people were already waiting. For two hours, Frances extended a gloved hand to people of "high and low degree," as one observer noted. At the end of the reception, she continued to smile warmly, insisting she wasn't a bit tired.

The staff was heartbroken that Mrs. Cleveland was leaving. On Inauguration Day, just before Frances and

✫ ✫ ✫ ✫ ✫ ✫ ✫ ✫ ✫ ✫ ✫ ✫ ✫ ✫ ✫ ✫

This photographic portrait of Frances Folsom Cleveland was taken in 1897.

Frances is shown here wearing a hat, possibly as she was leaving the White House for the last time.

her daughters were to leave for their new home in Princeton, New Jersey, she called the entire staff together to say goodbye. Frances thanked them for all their help, especially when she'd first arrived at the White House as "practically a girl." And then she broke down and "wept as if her heart would break."

Frances was very happy, at least, with the choice of the family's new home. She and Grover had agreed to settle in the lovely university town of Princeton, New Jersey. Grover Cleveland had made several close friends among the faculty during his presidency, notably Andrew West. Professor West had been a great source of comfort and solace to Grover during the last difficult months of his presidency. When the Clevelands bought their new house in Princeton—a large,

A bird's-eye view of the Princeton campus

Westland, the Clevelands' large, stuccoed colonial home in Princeton

Presidential Paths Cross at Princeton

✮ ✮

Princeton University is one of the four oldest colleges in the United States. Founded in 1746 as the College of New Jersey, it moved to Princeton in 1756. Nassau Hall, the oldest building on campus, dates to that year and was occupied by both British and colonial troops during the Revolutionary War. Since Richard Stockton, a member of the first graduating class and a signer of the Declaration of Independence, Princeton has continued to contribute to American political life. U.S. presidents James Madison and Woodrow Wilson graduated from Princeton. Before he went to Washington, Wilson headed the university from 1902 to 1910. During much of that time, Grover Cleveland served with his friend Andrew West on the college's board of trustees. He and West both disagreed with Wilson about where a new graduate school ought to be located. Wilson favored a central location on campus, while West and Cleveland felt it should be farther away and more isolated. When financial donors backed West's plan, Wilson gave in. And, while Cleveland named his home Westland after his friend, in a fitting twist, the college named the new clock tower at the graduate school the Grover Cleveland Memorial Tower.

Nassau Hall, the oldest building on the Princeton campus

stuccoed colonial—they named it Westland.

Even though Grover's political career was coming to an end, "retirement" hardly seemed the appropriate word for the next phase of his family's life. Grover wasn't yet sixty and Frances was only thirty-two. The couple had every hope that other children would join Ruth, Esther, and Marion, their third daughter who was born in 1895.

Grover Cleveland was indeed depressed and embittered at the end of his final term in office. He wanted to believe that he'd done the best for his country, but he was plagued with doubts. Evidence of his failures seemed everywhere. He and Frances hoped that, after several months of rest, he would be able to put his accomplishments into perspective.

Just after watching the inauguration of William McKinley, Cleveland exchanged a few words with the new president and then boarded a friend's fishing boat. With Frances's blessing, the former president and two friends headed off on a two-week fishing and hunting trip along the coast of North Carolina. His friends on board recalled how weary the president looked as he dropped himself into a deck chair and gave a huge sigh. A few days later, however, his appearance began to brighten.

By the time Grover arrived in Princeton, Frances and the children were already settled into their new

Frances and Grover Cleveland seated on the porch steps of their Princeton home, Westland

Grover Cleveland in his doctoral robes at Princeton

The couple's first son, Richard Folsom Cleveland, was born on November 11, 1897. A second son, Francis Grover Cleveland, was born on July 18, 1903. The proud father noted that Francis's four-year-old brother was "quite overcome with laughter when he found it was a 'real baby'."

Cleveland with his youngest son, Francis Grover

home. Within a few months, the transition into private life was successfully underway. The former president spent his days writing articles, preparing speeches, and meeting members of the university community. Many days, however, were spent happily in the company of Frances and his three daughters. One evening in 1897, he began a letter to a friend by noting: "Today was a pony day here. . . ."

Death of a Disease

★ ★

Thirteen-year-old Ruth Cleveland's death from diphtheria would be nearly unheard-of today. The disease, however, was once a much-feared killer of children. While it begins with bacteria in the throat, diphtheria's danger lies in the toxin it spreads through the body's bloodstream. This poison can cause the throat to swell up so that the patient is unable to breathe. It can also infect the heart muscle and paralyze the limbs. Diphtheria is a highly contagious disease transmitted by coughing and sneezing. Its germs linger on toys and other objects, making it especially threatening to children, who are often in close contact with one another. Although a treatment for people with the disease was discovered in Germany in 1890, the threat of diphtheria endured until the 1920s when large-scale immunization programs began. Today, infants are routinely vaccinated with just enough diphtheria toxin to strengthen their immunity to the disease without making them sick. As a result, diphtheria has all but disappeared in countries like the United States, while many developing nations still suffer its effects.

The happy home seemed complete. Unfortunately, however, in those days before modern medicine, no family was safe from the specter of sudden illness. On January 2, 1904, the oldest child, Ruth, became very ill with tonsillitis. Within a week, she had contracted diphtheria and then, suddenly, she was dead.

The family spent a long winter grieving, wondering how they could ever be happy again. When summer returned, they found they couldn't bear returning to Gray Gables on Buzzards Bay, the site of so many happy family gatherings. They sold the beloved house and bought a new one in Tamworth, New Hampshire, in the foothills of the White Mountains.

As Grover Cleveland celebrated his seventieth birthday on March 18, 1907, he was pleased that his reputa-

After Ruth's death, the Clevelands sold Gray Gables and bought this house in Tamworth, New Hampshire.

Tamworth is located in the foothills of the White Mountains (above).

Grover Cleveland is shown here gardening with his sons shortly before his death.

tion had been restored in the public's mind. The day even became something of a national celebration. The former president received cards, gifts, and tributes from all over the world

These words of praise gave Grover Cleveland great satisfaction, especially since he knew his health was failing. He wanted so much to be appreciated for at least trying to be a good, honest man. As he lay dying of heart and kidney failure on June 24, 1908,

Grover Cleveland toward the end of his life

Grover would have smiled at this out-pouring of affection. Yet he was a sensitive, humble man, and so Frances gladly followed his wish to have his gravestone read simply:

Grover Cleveland
Born Caldwell, N.J., March 18, 1837
Died Princeton, N.J., June 24, 1908

he spoke his final words: "I have tried so hard to do right."

President Theodore Roosevelt, members of his cabinet, Supreme Court justices, and members of Congress attended the funeral. James Russell Lowell, an eminent poet of the time, called Grover Cleveland the "most typical" American since Abraham Lincoln. Frances knew that

Poet James Russell Lowell called Cleveland the "most typical" American since Abraham Lincoln.

★ ★ ★ ★ ★ ★ ★ ★ ★ ★ ★ ★ ★ ★

CHAPTER SEVEN

Frances on Her Own

☆ ☆ ☆ ☆ ☆ ☆ ☆ ☆ ☆ ☆ ☆ ☆ ☆ ☆ ☆ ☆

Frances Folsom Cleveland had spent much of her adult life as a public figure; now she would truly begin to live as a private citizen. She was fortunate that her life in Princeton was very full and happy. She had a wonderful home and family, close friends, and she was a respected member of the community who contributed meaningfully to civic causes. At only forty-four, there was certainly no reason for her to slow down.

On January 11, 1913, Frances returned to the White House for a dinner held in her honor by President William Howard Taft and his wife, Nellie. They were eager for her to see all the changes in the mansion

☆ ☆ ☆ ☆ ☆ ☆ ☆ ☆ ☆ ☆ ☆ ☆ ☆ ☆ ☆ ☆

President William Howard Taft

since her departure, including the new East Terrace entrance and a First Ladies portrait gallery. From the terrace, she walked upstairs to the Blue Room, where she'd been married twenty-six years before. Observers noted that she was "deeply affected" by her brief visit.

Later in 1913, she surprised everyone all over again by remarrying—the first First Lady to do so. She wed Thomas J. Preston Jr., a professor of

A Welcoming Space

★ ★

The White House Blue Room, which figured so importantly in Frances's life, is among the most elegant of the 132 rooms in the mansion. Today, it is one of the rooms open to the public. Designed as the central reception room by the original White House architect in 1792, the large, oval Blue Room still welcomes guests today. Three large windows overlook the south lawn, or President's Park, and offer a striking view of the Washington Monument and the Jefferson Memorial. The room has been redecorated repeatedly over the years; President Martin Van Buren made it blue for the first time in 1837. During the Clevelands' time, lush potted plants, a huge chandelier, velvet upholstery, and a riotously mismatched selection of wallpaper and carpet patterns overwhelmed the space. While such lavish interior decorating was the fashion in the late nineteenth century, the lovely Blue Room has today been restored to the period from 1817 to 1825, when President Monroe furnished it to impress the world with America's good taste.

y Telegraph to The Tribune.]
on, N. J., Feb. 10.—Mrs. Frances
Cleveland and Thomas Jex Pres-
were married quietly here to-day
ject. President John Grier Hib-
Princeton University performed
mony. Owing to the recent ill-
Mr. Preston, the wedding was pri-
d, with the exception of Presi-
d Mrs. Hibben, Miss Elizabeth
and Dean Andrew West, none but
le members of the family were

*A newspaper article about the 1913 marriage
of Frances Cleveland to Thomas J. Preston Jr.*

*Frances and three of her children returning from a
trip to Switzerland in 1914*

archaeology at Wells College, who
would later teach at Princeton. Mr.
and Mrs. Preston led a contented life
in Princeton, surrounded by the
Cleveland children and many friends.
The whole clan looked forward every

summer to long, lazy stays at their summer home in Tamworth, New Hampshire.

Over the years, Frances became very involved in the cause of higher

This photograph of Frances Folsom Cleveland Preston was taken in 1928.

education for women. She served as a trustee for Wells College for more than a half century. She also actively lobbied the state of New Jersey to offer equal educational opportunities for women and was instrumental in the founding of the New Jersey College for Women.

Shortly after the end of World War II, Frances took part in a ceremony marking the anniversary of Princeton University. Harry Truman was president, and he, along with his wife Bess, former President Herbert Hoover, former First Lady Edith Wilson, General and Mrs. Dwight Eisenhower, attended the ceremony. President Truman delighted Frances by telling her how his own mother had traveled from their farm near Independence, Missouri, all the way to Kansas City just to catch a glimpse of the incomparable Frances Cleveland. Mrs. Truman had also preserved clippings about "Frankie," the most famous bride of the nineteenth century, in an old scrapbook the president still had in his possession.

Frances Cleveland Preston died on October 29, 1947, while visiting her

Left to right. First Lady Bess Truman, former First Lady Frances Cleveland Preston, President Truman, former President Herbert Hoover, and former First Lady Edith Wilson took part in a ceremony marking the anniversary of Princeton University.

oldest son, Richard, an attorney in Baltimore, for his fiftieth birthday celebration. According to her wishes, she was buried next to Grover Cleveland, "her beloved husband," in Princeton, New Jersey.

Frances Folsom Cleveland Preston in 1934

Portrait of America, 1947: No Place Like Home

☆ ☆

Born at the end of the Civil War, Frances died eighty-three years later. By 1947, soldiers and sailors returned home by the thousands from World War II. To make their homecomings happy, women left their wartime jobs to resume full-time homemaking. A million new homes were built. For a good many of America's nearly 150 million people, there was no place like home.

Times were good. The economy thrived as Americans around the forty-eight states resumed their peacetime lives under the presidency of Harry Truman. The baby boom was well underway as young couples joyously began married lives post-poned by half a decade of war. White families fled the cities in droves, seeking the American dream in the tidy new suburban communities that sprouted around the landscape. African-American families had far fewer chances at the dream since they were not generally welcome in these new residential enclaves.

American living rooms glowed with the electronic light of the latest advance in home entertainment—television. A freckle-faced puppet named Howdy Doody made his TV debut and became a lasting symbol of the times. All three networks carried the first-ever World Series broadcast: the New York Yankees beat the Brooklyn Dodgers four games to three. Jackie Robinson, the first African-American player admitted to the major leagues, played for Brooklyn. He was made 1947's Rookie of the Year but was repeatedly refused hotel rooms because of his skin color.

Teenagers, no longer living in the gloom of war, could finally enjoy their youth. Bobbysoxers gathered around jukeboxes to swoon over the music of young Frank Sinatra. Drive-in movies and soda fountains swarmed with legions of blue-jeaned teens escaping the watchful eye of parents. Bubble-gum-blowing contests took the country by storm.

Into the good times, however, crept a new phrase: *cold war*. The Cold War, a political and military standoff between the two world superpowers, the United States and the Communist USSR, settled in like a deep freeze. In spite of their prosperity and optimism, Americans lived in its chilly shadow, fearing Soviet expansion in Europe, the spread of Communism, and the threat of nuclear war.

While she would never know the Cold War, Frances's life had touched four major American conflicts—the Civil War, the Spanish-American War, and World Wars I and II—enough for any lifetime.

☆ ☆ ☆ ☆ ☆ ☆ ☆ ☆ ☆ ☆ ☆ ☆ ☆ ☆ ☆

The Presidents and Their First Ladies

YEARS IN OFFICE			
President	Birth–Death	First Lady	Birth–Death
1789–1797			
George Washington	1732–1799	Martha Dandridge Custis Washington	1731–1802
1797–1801			
John Adams	1735–1826	Abigail Smith Adams	1744–1818
1801–1809			
Thomas Jefferson†	1743–1826		
1809–1817			
James Madison	1751–1836	Dolley Payne Todd Madison	1768–1849
1817–1825			
James Monroe	1758–1831	Elizabeth Kortright Monroe	1768–1830
1825–1829			
John Quincy Adams	1767–1848	Louisa Catherine Johnson Adams	1775–1852
1829–1837			
Andrew Jackson†	1767–1845		
1837–1841			
Martin Van Buren†	1782–1862		
1841			
William Henry Harrison‡	1773–1841		
1841–1845			
John Tyler	1790–1862	Letitia Christian Tyler (1841–1842)	1790–1842
		Julia Gardiner Tyler (1844–1845)	1820–1889
1845–1849			
James K. Polk	1795–1849	Sarah Childress Polk	1803–1891
1849–1850			
Zachary Taylor	1784–1850	Margaret Mackall Smith Taylor	1788–1852
1850–1853			
Millard Fillmore	1800–1874	Abigail Powers Fillmore	1798–1853
1853–1857			
Franklin Pierce	1804–1869	Jane Means Appleton Pierce	1806–1863
1857–1861			
James Buchanan*	1791–1868		
1861–1865			
Abraham Lincoln	1809–1865	Mary Todd Lincoln	1818–1882
1865–1869			
Andrew Johnson	1808–1875	Eliza McCardle Johnson	1810–1876
1869–1877			
Ulysses S. Grant	1822–1885	Julia Dent Grant	1826–1902
1877–1881			
Rutherford B. Hayes	1822–1893	Lucy Ware Webb Hayes	1831–1889
1881			
James A. Garfield	1831–1881	Lucretia Rudolph Garfield	1832–1918
1881–1885			
Chester A. Arthur†	1829–1886		

† wife died before he took office   ‡ wife too ill to accompany him to Washington   * never married

1885–1889			
Grover Cleveland	1837–1908	Frances Folsom Cleveland	1864–1947
1889–1893			
Benjamin Harrison	1833–1901	Caroline Lavinia Scott Harrison	1832–1892
1893–1897			
Grover Cleveland	1837–1908	Frances Folsom Cleveland	1864–1947
1897–1901			
William McKinley	1843–1901	Ida Saxton McKinley	1847–1907
1901–1909			
Theodore Roosevelt	1858–1919	Edith Kermit Carow Roosevelt	1861–1948
1909–1913			
William Howard Taft	1857–1930	Helen Herron Taft	1861–1943
1913–1921			
Woodrow Wilson	1856–1924	Ellen Louise Axson Wilson (1913–1914)	1860–1914
		Edith Bolling Galt Wilson (1915–1921)	1872–1961
1921–1923			
Warren G. Harding	1865–1923	Florence Kling Harding	1860–1924
1923–1929			
Calvin Coolidge	1872–1933	Grace Anna Goodhue Coolidge	1879–1957
1929–1933			
Herbert Hoover	1874–1964	Lou Henry Hoover	1874–1944
1933–1945			
Franklin D. Roosevelt	1882–1945	Anna Eleanor Roosevelt	1884–1962
1945–1953			
Harry S. Truman	1884–1972	Bess Wallace Truman	1885–1982
1953–1961			
Dwight D. Eisenhower	1890–1969	Mamie Geneva Doud Eisenhower	1896–1979
1961–1963			
John F. Kennedy	1917–1963	Jacqueline Bouvier Kennedy	1929–1994
1963–1969			
Lyndon B. Johnson	1908–1973	Claudia Taylor (Lady Bird) Johnson	1912–
1969–1974			
Richard Nixon	1913–1994	Patricia Ryan Nixon	1912–1993
1974–1977			
Gerald Ford	1913–	Elizabeth Bloomer Ford	1918–
1977–1981			
James Carter	1924–	Rosalynn Smith Carter	1927–
1981–1989			
Ronald Reagan	1911–	Nancy Davis Reagan	1923–
1989–1993			
George Bush	1924–	Barbara Pierce Bush	1925–
1993–			
William Jefferson Clinton	1946–	Hillary Rodham Clinton	1947–

Frances Folsom Cleveland
Timeline

1864	★	Frances Folsom is born on July 21
		Abraham Lincoln is reelected president
1865	★	Civil War ends
		Abraham Lincoln is assassinated
		Andrew Johnson becomes president
1866	★	Final transatlantic cable is laid between Great Britain and the United States
1868	★	Ulysses S. Grant is elected president
1869	★	National Women Suffrage Association is formed
1871	★	Fire destroys most of Chicago
1872	★	Susan B. Anthony is arrested for trying to vote
		Ulysses S. Grant is reelected president
		Yellowstone National Park becomes the first U.S. national park
1873	★	Economic depression spreads throughout the United States
1877	★	Rutherford B. Hayes becomes president
		Thomas Edison patents the phonograph
1878	★	First bicycles are manufactured in the United States
1879	★	Women win the right to argue cases before the Supreme Court
1880	★	James A. Garfield is elected president
1881	★	James A. Garfield is shot and dies about three months later
		Chester A. Arthur becomes president
1882	★	Congress approves a pension for widows of U.S. presidents

1883	★	Brooklyn Bridge opens
		First baseball game under electric lights is played
1884	★	Grover Cleveland is elected president
1885	★	Washington Monument is dedicated
		Frances Folsom graduates from Wells College
1886	★	President Cleveland dedicates the Statue of Liberty
		American Federation of Labor is organized
		Frances Folsom marries Grover Cleveland in the White House
1887	★	Interstate Commerce Commission is established
1888	★	Benjamin Harrison is elected president
		George Eastman introduces the Kodak camera
1889	★	Oklahoma is opened to non-Native American settlers
		Flood in Johnstown, Pennsylvania, kills 2,295 people
1891	★	Joe Naismith invents basketball
		Ruth Cleveland is born
1892	★	Ellis Island immigration center opens
		Grover Cleveland is elected president
1893	★	Women's suffrage is adopted in Colorado
		Economic depression hits the United States
		Esther Cleveland is born in the White House
1895	★	Marion Cleveland is born
1896	★	First Ford automobile is built in Detroit
		First modern Olympics are held in Athens, Greece
		William McKinley is elected president
1897	★	First Boston Marathon is run
		Richard Folsom Cleveland is born
1900	★	William McKinley is reelected president
1901	★	President McKinley is assassinated
		Theodore Roosevelt becomes president

1903	★	Panama and the United States sign a treaty for the building of the Panama Canal
		Wright brothers fly their airplane for the first time
		First World Series is played
		Francis Grover Cleveland is born
1904	★	Theodore Roosevelt is elected president
		Ruth Cleveland dies
1906	★	Theodore Roosevelt receives the Nobel Peace Prize
1908	★	Grover Cleveland dies
		William Howard Taft is elected president
1909	★	National Association for the Advancement of Colored People (NAACP) is founded
1910	★	Boy Scouts of America is founded
1911	★	First Indianapolis 500 is held
1912	★	Woodrow Wilson is elected president
		Titanic sinks in the North Atlantic
1913	★	Frances Folsom Cleveland marries Thomas J. Preston
		Henry Ford sets up his first assembly line
1914	★	Panama Canal is completed
		World War I begins
1916	★	Woodrow Wilson is reelected president
		National Park Service is established
1917	★	United States enters World War I
1918	★	United States and its allies win World War I
1920	★	Nineteenth Amendment, which gives women the right to vote, is added to the Constitution
		Warren G. Harding is elected president
		Woodrow Wilson receives the Nobel Peace Prize
1922	★	First woman is appointed to the U.S. Senate
		Lincoln Memorial is dedicated
1923	★	President Harding dies
		Calvin Coolidge becomes president

1924	★	Calvin Coolidge is elected president First Winter Olympic Games are held
1925	★	First National Spelling Bee is held
1927	★	Charles Lindbergh flies solo across the Atlantic Ocean
1928	★	Herbert Hoover is elected president
1929	★	Stock market crashes, starting the Great Depression
1931	★	"The Star-Spangled Banner" becomes the national anthem
1932	★	Amelia Earhart becomes the first woman to fly solo across the Atlantic Ocean First woman is elected to the U.S. Senate Franklin D. Roosevelt is elected president
1933	★	President Roosevelt begins the New Deal
1934	★	Scientist at the DuPont Company invents nylon
1935	★	Congress passes the Social Security Act
1936	★	Franklin D. Roosevelt is reelected president
1937	★	Golden Gate Bridge is dedicated in San Francisco
1939	★	World War II begins
1940	★	Franklin D. Roosevelt is reelected president
1941	★	Japanese bomb Pearl Harbor United States enters World War II
1944	★	Franklin D. Roosevelt is reelected president
1945	★	President Roosevelt dies Harry S. Truman becomes president Germany surrenders to the Allies in Europe United States drops atomic bombs on Japan Japan surrenders, ending World War II
1947	★	Frances Folsom Cleveland Preston dies on October 27

Fast Facts about
Frances Folsom Cleveland

Born: July 21, 1864, in Buffalo, New York

Died: October 27, 1947, in Baltimore, Maryland

Burial Site: Princeton, New Jersey

Parents: Oscar Folsom and Emma Harmon Folsom

Education: Madame Breckner's French Kindergarten and Miss Bissel's School for Young Ladies in Buffalo; Wheaton School in St. Paul, Minnesota; high schools in Medina and Buffalo, New York; graduated from Wells College in Aurora, New York (1885)

First Marriage: To Grover Cleveland on June 2, 1886, until his death on June 24, 1908

Second Marriage: To Thomas J. Preston on February 10, 1913

Children: Ruth (1891–1904), Esther, Marion, Richard Folsom, Francis Grover

Places She Lived: Buffalo, New York (1864–1876, 1878–1885); St. Paul, Minnesota (1876–1877); Medina, New York (1877–1878); Aurora, New York (1882–1885); Washington, D.C. (1885–1889, 1893–1897); New York City (1889–1893); Princeton, New Jersey (1897–1947); with summer homes at Folsomdale in New York; Buzzards Bay, Massachusetts; and Tamworth, New Hampshire

Major Achievements:

  * Became the youngest First Lady and the first First Lady to be married in the White House.
  * Held large daytime receptions during the week and began Saturday afternoon receptions so that working women could visit the White House.
  * Gave birth to the only child of a president born in the White House.
  * Served as a trustee for Wells College for about fifty years.
  * Lobbied the state of New Jersey to provide equal educational opportunities for women.
  * Helped found the New Jersey College for Women.

Fast Facts about
Grover Cleveland's Presidency

Terms of Office: Elected in 1884 and 1892; served as the twenty-second president of the United States from 1885 to 1889 and as the twenty-fourth president from 1893 to 1897, the only president to serve two terms that were not consecutive.

Vice Presidents: Thomas Hendricks from March 4, 1885, until his death on November 25, 1885; Adlai E. Stevenson from March 4, 1893, to March 4, 1897.

Major Policy Decisions and Legislation:

* Put the Pendleton Civil Service Act into effect by opening thousands of federal government jobs to merit selection of employees.

* Vetoed private pension bills for individual Civil War veterans (1886).

* Favored lowering the tariff but was unsuccessful at convincing Congress to do so (1886 and 1887).

* Successfully convinced Congress to repeal the Sherman Silver Purchase Act (1893).

* Sent federal troops to break up the Pullman Strike in Chicago (May 1894).

* Withdrew a treaty that would have annexed the Hawaiian Islands to the United States (1893).

Major Events:

* President Cleveland dedicated the Statue of Liberty on October 28, 1886.

* President Cleveland appointed the following to the U.S. Supreme Court: Melville Weston Fuller as chief justice and Lucius Quintus Cincinnatus Lamar as an associate justice (1888); Edward White (1894) and Rufus Peckham (1895) as associate justices.

* The Panic of 1893 started a depression throughout the United States.

* President Cleveland officially opened the World's Columbian Exposition (Chicago World's Fair) on May 1, 1893.

* Workers at the Pullman Company in Chicago went on strike, leading to a railroad strike throughout the Midwest (1894).

* Hawaii became a republic on July 4, 1894.

* Utah was admitted as the forty-fifth state on January 4, 1896.

Where to Visit

The Capitol Building
Constitution Avenue
Washington, D.C. 20510
(202) 225-3121

Museum of American History of the Smithsonian Institution
"First Ladies: Political and Public Image"
14th Street and Constitution Avenue, NW
Washington, D.C.
(202) 357-2008

National Archives
Constitution Avenue
Washington, D.C.
(202) 501-5000

The National First Ladies Library
The Saxton McKinley House
331 S. Market Avenue
Canton, Ohio 44702

White House
1600 Pennsylvania Avenue
Washington, D.C. 20500
Visitor's Office: (202) 456-7041

White House Historical Association
740 Jackson Place NW
Washington, D.C. 20503
(202) 737-8292

Online Sites of Interest

The First Ladies of the United States of America
http://www2.whitehouse.gov/WH/glimpse/firstladies/html/firstladies.html
A portrait and biographical sketch of each First Lady plus links to other White House sites

Grolier Online: The American Presidency
http://www.grolier.com/presidents/nbk/bios/22pclev.html
An extensive biography with links to Cleveland's inaugural address, quick facts on Cleveland and his presidency,, other presidents, and more

History Happens
http://www.usahistory.com/presidents
A site that contains fast facts about Grover Cleveland, including personal information and Inaugural Address

Internet Public Library, Presidents of the United States (IPL POTUS)
http://www.ipl.org/ref/POTUS/gcleveland.html
A site with much information on Grover Cleveland, including personal information and facts about his presidency;

many links to other sites including biographies and other Internet resources

The National First Ladies Library
http://www.firstladies.org
The first virtual library devoted to the lives and legacies of America's First Ladies; includes a bibliography of books, articles, letters, and manuscripts by and about the nation's First Ladies; also includes a virtual tour, with pictures, of the restored Saxton McKinley House in Canton, Ohio, which houses the library

The White House
http://www.whitehouse.gov/WH/Welcome.html
Information about the current president and vice president; White House history and tours; biographies of past presidents and their families; a tour of the historic building, current events, and much more

The White House for Kids
http://www.whitehouse.gov/WH/kids/html/kidshome.html
Includes information about White House kids, past and present; famous "First Pets," past and present; historic moments of the presidency; and more

For Further Reading

Gormley, Beatrice. *First Ladies*. New York: Scholastic, Inc., 1997.

Gould, Lewis L. (ed.). *American First Ladies: Their Lives and Their Legacy*. New York: Garland Publishing, 1996.

Guzzetti, Paula. *The White House*. Parsippany, N.J.: Silver Burdett Press, 1995.

Jacobson, Doranne. *Presidents and First Ladies of the United States*. New York: Smithmark Publishers, Inc., 1995.

Kent, Zachary. *Grover Cleveland: Twenty-Second and Twenty-Fourth President of the United States*. Encyclopedia of Presidents series. Chicago: Childrens Press, 1988.

Klapthor, Margaret Brown. *The First Ladies*. 8th edition. Washington, D.C.: White House Historical Association, 1995.

Mayo, Edith P. (ed.). *The Smithsonian Book of the First Ladies: Their Lives, Times, and Issues*. New York: Henry Holt, 1996.

Index

Page numbers in **boldface type** indicate illustrations

Cleveland, Frances Folsom
(*continued*)
in Princeton, N.J., **78**, 80,
83–84, **88**, 89, 91, 93,
93
as private citizen, 63,
89–92
proposal from Grover
Cleveland, 42
relationship with father, 22
relationship with Uncle
Cleve, 20, 22
return to Medina, 25
with Ruth, **64**
social life of, 26
timeline for, 98–101
visit to Albany, New York,
Governor's Mansion, 31,
33
visit to the White House,
42
wedding dress of, **8**, 13, 15,
15, 16, **52**, 53, **53**
at Wells College, 18, 26,
27, 29–30, **30**, 33, 42
at Westland, **78**, 80, 83,
83
as White House hostess,
41, 54, **54**, **56**, 57, **61**,
76, 79
White House wedding of,
9–11, 13, 15, **15**, 16, 45,
52, 53, **53**
Cleveland, Francis Grover
(son), **78**, 84, **84**, **86**
Cleveland, Grover, **26**, **62**,
87
and birth of Frances, 20, 22

and birth of Ruth, 64
cancer surgery of, 67,
70–72
at Columbian Exposition,
68
courtship of Frances, 33–34
and death of Ruth, 85
description of, 10, 19, 22,
40, 42, 83, 87
and economic policies,
66–67
in election of 1884, 12, 34,
36, 37, **37**, 39
in election of 1888, 57–58,
60
and election of 1892, 64,
65–66, **65**
engagement to Frances, 9,
43, 47
failing health of, 86–87
fast facts about, 103
and Frances's engagement
to Charles Townsend,
26–27
friendship with Oscar
Folsom, 19–20, 24
funeral of, 87
as governor of New York,
31, 33, 34, 37
at Gray Gables, 57
as guardian for Frances, 24,
26–27
honeymoon of, 53–54
inaugurations of, **39**, 66,
66, **67**
and labor movement, 73,
75
legal practice of, 19, **20**, 63

love for fishing, 65–66, 83
move to Princeton, N.J.,
80, 83, **83**, 84, **84**
at New York city Memorial
Day parade, 49–50
at Oak View, **56**
political career of, 22
popularity of, 75–76
as president, 40, 52, 66–67,
68, 72–73, 75, 76–77
press coverage of, 11–12,
44, 53–54, 58, 72, 75, 76
at Princeton University,
80, 82, **84**
private life of, 11–12, 37,
63, 84
proposal to Frances by, 42
retirement from politics,
77
rise to national promi-
nence, 34
seventieth birthday cele-
bration for, 85–86
and the Sherman Silver
Purchase Act, 66–67, 73
sister Rose as official
White House hostess for,
40, 41, **41**, 42
with sons, 84, **84**, **86**
temper of, 12, 58
as Uncle Cleve, 20, 22
at Westland, **78**, 82, **83**
White House wedding of,
9–10, 45, **52**, 53, **53**
Cleveland, Grover, Memorial
Tower, 82
Cleveland, Marion (daugh-
ter), **78**, 83

108

M

Madame Breckner's French
    Kindergarten, 23, 24
Madison, Dolley, 13, 41
Madison, James, 82
Marine Band, 13, 14, **14**
McKinley, William, 77, **77,**
    83
Medina, New York, 23, 24,
    26
The Mikado, 50, 51
Miss Bissel's School for
    Young Ladies, 23, 24
Monroe, James, 90

N

Nassau Hall, 82, **82**
Native Americans, 17
New Jersey College for
    Women, 92
New York City, 21, 38, 39,
    44, 45, 47, 49–50, **49,**
    50, 52, 63, 70
New York City Memorial
    Day Parade, 49–50, 52
New York State, 21
    Governor's Mansion in, 31,
    31
    State Capitol in, **32**
Niagara Falls, 21, **21**

O

Oak View, **56**
Oneida (yacht), 70–71, **70**

P

Pierce, Jane Appleton, 41
The Pirates of Penzance, 51

political machines, 34, 38,
    38
presidents, listing of, 96–97
press, power of, 12, 38
Preston, Thomas J. Jr.,
    90–91, **91**
Princeton, N.J., 80, **81,**
    83–84
Princeton University, 80, **81,**
    82, **82, 84,** 91, 92
Pulitzer, Joseph, 12
Pullman Company, 73, **74,**
    75

R

Republicans, 37, 57, 60, 77
Robinson, Jackie, 94
Roosevelt, Franklin, 71
Roosevelt, Theodore, 87

S

St. Gaudens, Augustus, **75**
St. Paul, Minnesota, 25, **25**
Sherman Silver Purchase
    Act, 66–67, 73
Smith, Helen Fairchild,
    29–30, **30,** 54
Sousa, John Philip, 13, 14,
    14
Sullivan, Arthur, 50, 51

T

Taft, Nellie, 89
Taft, William Howard, 89,
    90
Tammany Hall, 38, 39, **66**
Tamworth, New Hampshire,
    85, **86,** 92

Thurman, Allen G., 60
Townsend, Charles, 26–27
Truman, Bess, 92, **93**
Truman, Harry, 92, **93,** 94
Tweed, William Marcy
    (Boss), 7, 38, **38**

V

Van Buren, Martin, 90
Victoria, Queen of England,
    15, 53

W

Washington, D.C., **10,** 40,
    40, 42, 52, 57, 70, 73, 77
Washington, Martha, 41
Washington Monument, **40,**
    42, 90
Wells College, **26,** 27,
    29–30, **30,** 33, 42–43,
    54, 91, 92
West, Andrew, 80, 82
Westland, **78, 81,** 82, 83, **83**
Wheaton School, 25
White House, 10, 11, **11,** 13,
    15, **15,** 16, **16,** 42, 45,
    52, 53, 57, **59,** 61, 61,
    72, 90
    receptions at, 41, 54, **54,**
    56, 57, 76, 79
    State Dining Room, 16, **56**
Wilson, Edith, 92, **93**
Wilson, Woodrow, 82
women
    education for, 27, 40, 55,
    92
    receptions at White House
    for, 54, 79

Photo Identifications

Cover: Official White House portrait of Frances Folsom Cleveland
Page 8: Frances Folsom Cleveland in her wedding dress
Page 18: Frances as a college woman
Page 28: Frances Folsom and her mother, Emma Harmon Folsom
Page 46: Frances Folsom at about the time of her marriage to Grover Cleveland
Page 62: Official White House portraits of President Grover Cleveland and First Lady Frances Folsom Cleveland
Page 78: The Cleveland family, in retirement, on the porch steps of their New Jersey home
Page 88: Frances at her desk in Princeton, New Jersey

Photo Credits©

White House Historical Association— cover, 54, 62 (bottom); photograph by the National Geographic, 62 (top), 98 (top)

Wells College Archives, Louis Jefferson Long Library, Aurora, New York— 8, 26 (right), 28, 30 (both pictures), 91 (left)

North Wind Picture Archives— 10 (both pictures), 25, 31 (top), 37 (bottom), 39 (top), 56 (top), 67 (top), 73, 74 (top and bottom right), 75 (left), 76 (both pictures), 77 (bottom), 84 (both pictures)

Stock Montage, Inc.— 11, 16, 21, 31 (bottom), 32 (bottom), 35 (top), 36 (top), 40 (top left and right), 45, 49 (top), 56 (bottom), 58 (top), 69 (bottom left and right), 101 (top)

Archive Photos— 14 (left), 20 (bottom), 34, 35 (bottom), 36 (bottom left), 38, 39 (bottom), 46, 48, 50 (bottom), 87 (left); Kean, 13, 18, 32 (top), 37 (top), 50 (top), 68 (both pictures), 69 (top), 80 (left), 86 (bottom); Museum of the City of New York/Kean, 80 (right)

AP/Wide World Photos— 14 (right), 26 (left), 40 (bottom), 72, 92, 93 (bottom), 101 (bottom)

North Wind Pictures— 15, 49 (bottom left and right), 60

Buffalo and Erie County Historical Society— 20 (top), 22, 23 (both pictures)

Corbis-Bettmann— 36 (bottom left), 52 (left), 53, 58 (bottom), 64 (right), 65, 66 (both pictures), 67 (bottom), 70 (both pictures), 74 (bottom left), 77 (top), 81 (top), 87 (right), 88, 90, 100 (top); Underwood & Underwood, 78; UPI, 81 (bottom), 83, 91 (right), 93 (top), 100 (bottom)

Reproduced from the Collections of the Library of Congress— 41, 59 (bottom), 75 (right)

New England Stock Photos— Clyde H. Smith, 42, 43; J. L. Rezendes, 86 (top right)

Culver Pictures, Inc.— 51

The Smithsonian Institution— 52 (right)

Bourne Archives— 57

Collection of the New York Historical Society— 59 (top), 64 (left), 99

Princeton University Libraries Special Collections— 82

Courtesy Steve Damon— 86 (top left)

SuperStock International, Inc.— 98 (bottom)

About the Author

Susan Sinnott began her publishing career as an editor for *Cricket*, a literary magazine for children. She later worked for the University of Wisconsin Press, where she managed and edited academic journals. Eventually, her own children pulled her away from scholarly publishing and helped her rediscover the joys of reading and writing books for young people. Ms. Sinnott's books include a previous Encyclopedia of First Ladies book, *Sarah Childress Polk* as well as *Extraordinary Hispanic Americans* and *Extraordinary Asian Pacific Americans* for Children's Press; and *Chinese Railroad Workers* and *Doing Our Part: American Women on the Home Front During World War II* for Franklin Watts.